NORTHERN IRELAND

SIMON ADAMS

W

FRANKLIN WATTS
LONDON•SYDNEY

For Tom, who should know this history already

Designer Steve Prosser
Editor Belinda Hollyer
Art Director Jonathan Hair
Editor-in-Chief John C. Miles
Picture Research Diana Morris
Map artwork Ian Thompson

© 2004 Franklin Watts

First published in 2004
by Franklin Watts
96 Leonard Street
London
EC2A 4XD

Franklin Watts Australia
45-51 Huntley Street
Alexandria
NSW 2015

ISBN 0 7496 5541 0

A CIP catalogue record for this book is
available from the British Library.

Printed in Malaysia

Picture credits
AP/Topham: 33, 35
Nicholas Bailey/Rex Features: front cover t, 28
Bettmann/Corbis: front cover b, 31
British Library/HIP/Topham: 17
Corbis: 19
Richard Cummins/Corbis: 41
Hulton Archive: 12
Hulton Deutsch/Corbis: 26
PA/Topham: back cover, 24, 37, 38
Picturepoint/Topham: 8, 10, 13, 14, 15, 16, 18, 20, 21, 22, 23, 29, 30, 34
PressNet/Topham: 39
Ron Sachs/Rex Features: 36

Every attempt has been made to clear copyright. Should there be any inadvertent omission, please apply to the publisher for rectification.

CONTENTS

INTRODUCTION

For more than 30 years, the 'Troubles' in Northern Ireland have kept this small corner of Europe on the world stage, and given it a reputation for violence, bigotry and hatred. But what is the background to the Troubles, and what has caused them?

THE ISLAND OF IRELAND

Ireland lies off the northwest coast of Europe, the smaller of the two main British Isles. It is traditionally divided into four provinces - Ulster, Leinster, Munster and Connacht - and 32 separate counties.

The island has a coastal rim of mountains and hills that surrounds a central lowland of lakes, peat bogs and gently rolling pasture. The Gaelic language is still spoken in the far west and northwest of Ireland, but most Irish people now speak English.

The landscape of Northern Ireland is predominantly rural. There are not many major towns.

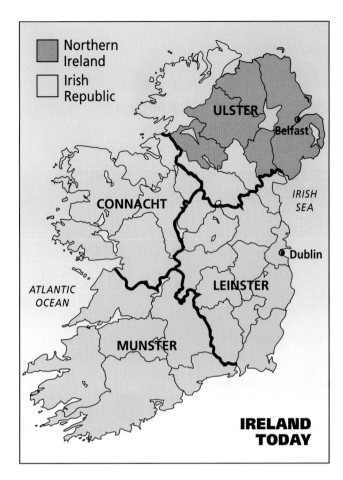

Northern Ireland
Irish Republic

ULSTER
Belfast
CONNACHT
IRISH SEA
Dublin
LEINSTER
ATLANTIC OCEAN
MUNSTER

IRELAND TODAY

IRISH LABELS

The various labels Irish people use to describe themselves and their religious and political beliefs can be confusing. In the heated politics of the province, none of the labels is neutral. Any of them can be a term of pride for one person and a term of abuse for another. The main labels used in this book are:

Roman Catholic A Christian who follows the authority of the Pope in Rome.

Protestant A Christian whose church broke with the Roman Catholic church during the Reformation of the 16th century, or was founded later.

Presbyterian A member of an independent, self-governing Protestant church.

Nationalist Someone who believes in an independent and united Ireland, achieved by consent.

Republican An extreme nationalist who favours an independent 32-county republic, achieved by violence if necessary.

Unionist Someone who believes in the union of all or part of Ireland with Britain, under the British crown.

Loyalist An extreme unionist who considers themself loyal to the British crown.

Most Irish are Roman Catholic, though in Ulster, the majority are Protestant.

Ireland was ruled by Britain for many years. In 1801 it was united with Britain, as the United Kingdom of Great Britain and Ireland. Then, in 1920, Ireland was divided. Six of the nine Ulster counties formed a new province of Northern Ireland, governed from Belfast, and remained part of the United Kingdom. The other 26 counties became a free state within the British Commonwealth, governed from Dublin. In 1949 those 26 counties became the independent Republic of Ireland. In 2001, 3,626,100 people lived in the Irish Republic, and 1,685,300 in Northern Ireland.

THE FLASHPOINT

The division of Ireland in 1920 - known as partition - was the result of a violent campaign for Irish Home Rule, that had split the island into two warring camps. The mostly Catholic nationalists and republicans wanted Home Rule or independence, while the mostly Protestant unionists and loyalists wanted to stay part of the United Kingdom (see the box above). But partition did not pacify the island, for many on both sides of the new border rejected it altogether. This rejection eventually led to the violent flashpoint of 1969, the backdrop to the current troubles in Northern Ireland.

ENGLAND AND IRELAND

Ireland was one of the last parts of Europe to be settled. The first people arrived – probably across a now sunken land bridge – from Britain only about 9,000 years ago. Around 500 BC, the Celts (originally from Germany) settled in Ireland. They introduced the Celtic language, the ancestor of modern-day Gaelic as well as of Welsh and Breton.

CHRISTIAN IRELAND

Ireland never became part of the Roman Empire, although French Christian missionaries reached the island in the late 4th or early 5th centuries AD. In 431 Palladius, a French priest, was appointed the first bishop to 'the Irish who believe in Christ'. St Patrick, a Roman citizen from England, arrived the next year to convert the Irish to Christianity. Irish history begins with St Patrick, for the first two written texts in Irish history are both by him. Christianity soon took hold, and Irish monks produced fine illuminated manuscripts, while missionaries travelled from here to other parts of Britain.

THE ENGLISH INVASION

Ireland was united by religion, but it still had many separate kingdoms. From 795 these were constantly threatened by Viking invaders from Scandinavia. A number of kings claimed to be high-king of all Ireland, most famously Brian Boru (died 1014), the king of Munster and also, because of his success in battle, the overlord of most of Ireland.

At this stage the main links with England were through the church and trade. But in 1166 Diarmait Mac Murchada, the king of Leinster, lost his throne and fled into exile in England. He appealed to King Henry II of England (reigned 1154-89) for help in recapturing his kingdom, promising in return to accept Henry as his overlord.

A small English force landed in Ireland in 1167 and another in 1169. Then, in 1170, a much larger army was sent, commanded by Richard de Clare, earl of Pembroke,

The Book of Kells was probably created by monks on the Scottish island of Iona in about AD 800, and brought for safekeeping to Ireland in 802.

THE PALE

At first, the English colonisation of Ireland was successful. English control spread out from towns, and land was taken from the Irish and given to English settlers. English common law and the English system of local government were introduced. Powerful Anglo-Irish families controlled the country and its parliament. But Irish resistance, Anglo-Irish rebellion, and English mismanagement meant that by the mid-1400s English rule was reduced to the area around Dublin known as the English Pale. The native Irish were largely left alone 'beyond the Pale'. When the Irish parliament recognised a rival claimant to his throne, King Henry VII of England (reigned 1485-1509) appointed Sir Edward Poynings lord deputy to push new laws through the Irish parliament. The laws stated that the lord deputy could not summon parliament without the king's permission, and that no law could be passed without royal approval. This greatly increased English royal control over Ireland.

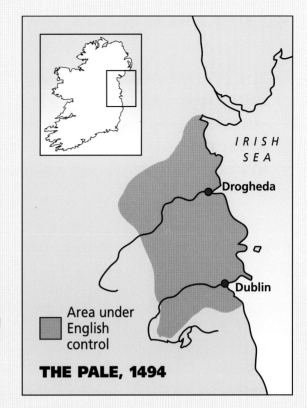

THE PALE, 1494

Area under English control

known as 'Strongbow'. Strongbow captured Dublin and through marriage inherited the kingdom of Leinster. His power was so great it threatened to rival King Henry's.

Henry II was alarmed by this development. In 1171 he went to Ireland himself, and secured recognition from many Irish kings as well as the Irish bishops as their overlord. From now on, the histories of England and Ireland were closely linked.

> '... those who are sent from England to govern them, who have little knowledge of the land of Ireland, ...use their offices to support themselves by extortion.'
>
> **Complaint in the Irish parliament, 1341**

EARLY IRISH HISTORY

c7000 BC First people settle in Ireland

c4000 BC First agricultural communities

c3000-2400 BC Stone Age burial tombs constructed

c500 BC Celts reach Ireland from Britain

AD 431 Palladius first Irish bishop of the Roman Catholic church

432 Traditional date for arrival of St Patrick to convert the Irish to Christianity

795 First Viking raid on Ireland

800 Monks produce Book of Kells, one

of the finest illuminated manuscripts

841 Vikings establish a permanent settlement on the site of the modern city of Dublin

1014 Death of Brian Boru, most powerful of Irish high-kings

1166 Diarmait Mac Murchada, king of Leinster, flees into

exile in England

1170 Strongbow invades Ireland

1171-72 Henry II leads expedition to Ireland

1264 First recorded meeting of Irish parliament

1494 Poynings' Law strengthens English control over Ireland

PLANTATION IRELAND

In 1534 Henry VIII broke with the Roman Catholic Church because the pope would not grant him a divorce. Henry declared himself supreme head of a new English church. Although the English Reformation was imposed on Ireland, too, most Irish remained loyal to Rome, creating tensions between the two countries.

KING OF IRELAND

In 1534 'Silken Thomas' Kildare, the lord deputy's son, rose in revolt against the government of the English King Henry VIII (reigned 1509-47). Kildare proclaimed a Catholic Crusade against Henry's new religion. The revolt was easily crushed but Henry imposed military rule, enforced the new church's doctrines and closed many Irish monasteries. In 1541 he changed his title from Lord to King of Ireland. Relations between Irish and English deteriorated for the rest of the Tudor period, and frequent revolts took place.

During the reign of Elizabeth I (1558-1603), the English church became increasingly Protestant. In 1593 rebellion broke out in Ulster, then the most Catholic part of Ireland. Led by Hugh O'Neill, with support from Catholic Spain, the rebel army had huge success before it was finally defeated at Kinsale, in County Cork, in 1601.

Rebel leader Hugh O'Neill, earl of Tyrone

PLANTATIONS AND CIVIL WAR

Throughout the Tudor period, Irish-held lands were taken away as punishment for rebellion, and given to English colonists to settle and farm as plantations. After O'Neill's rebellion, yet more plantations were established in Ulster, colonised by English Protestants and Scots Presbyterians. The City of London played a major financial role in this, rebuilding Derry and renaming it Londonderry. Catholicism was still tolerated in Ireland, but the purpose of these plantations was to outnumber the Catholic Irish population with new Protestant settlers.

The Stuart kings who followed Elizabeth were kings of three countries - England, Scotland and Ireland - and they found it hard to balance all three interests. The hardline religious policies of Charles I (reigned 1625-49) deeply offended Irish Catholics, who rose in revolt in 1641.

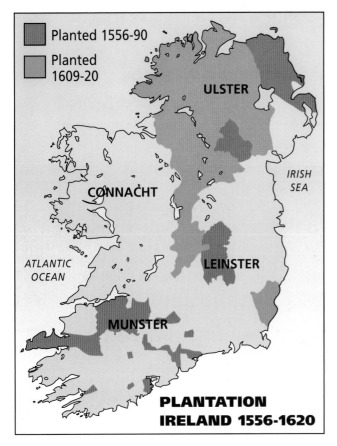

Planted 1556-90

Planted 1609-20

ULSTER

CONNACHT

IRISH SEA

ATLANTIC OCEAN

LEINSTER

MUNSTER

PLANTATION IRELAND 1556-1620

The rebels - the Confederate Catholics of Ireland - organised elections to an assembly in Kilkenny, from which Protestants were excluded (the only attempt at Irish self-rule until 1919). Charles was eventually forced to make peace because civil war had broken out in Britain, but the Confederates still controlled Ireland eight years later, when King Charles was executed by the English parliament.

CROMWELL IN IRELAND

In August 1649 the victorious English parliament sent their most successful general, Oliver Cromwell (1599-1658) to subdue Ireland. Cromwell besieged and sacked Drogheda, killing its royalist garrison and some of its citizens and priests. Further brutal sieges were conducted against other towns. Most of Ireland was under his control by May 1650 and all resistance was crushed by mid-1652. This left an intense legacy of bitterness against English rule in general and Cromwell in particular. Catholicism was suppressed and Protestants gained almost complete control over land, cities, trade and politics. The dispossessed Irish Catholics, transported west of the River Shannon to Connacht, were left with little.

TUDOR AND STUART IRELAND

1534 Henry VIII becomes head of the English church

1541 Henry VIII becomes king of Ireland

1556 Irish lands given to English colonists

1593 O'Neill family rebels against English rule, starting the Nine Years' War

1601 Spanish lands army in Cork; O'Neill and Spanish army heavily defeated

1604 Ulster divided into nine counties

1607 Flight of 100 Irish Catholic lords to Rome

1609 Ulster plantations established

1610 City of London Corporation agrees to rebuild Derry

1633-40 Charles I pursues hardline policies in Ireland

1641 Irish Catholics rise against Charles

1642 Confederate Catholics of Ireland call an assembly at Kilkenny

1643 English truce with Confederates

1649 Charles I executed by English parliament

1649-50 Cromwell brutally puts down Confederate rebellion

1652 Act of Settlement displaces Irish Catholics to Connacht

THE PROTESTANT ASCENDANCY

Although Cromwell's harsh land settlement was later revised, Ireland had to endure yet more conflict before Protestant supremacy was secured.

A NEW SETTLEMENT

In 1653, after his military success in Ireland, Oliver Cromwell became Lord Protector - a sort of military dictator. But after Cromwell's death the monarchy was restored. Charles I's son - Charles II - came to the throne in 1660. A new Act of Settlement for Ireland softened some elements of its predecessor. Even so, although about three-fifths of the land was Catholic-owned in 1642, only one-fifth was still in Catholic hands twenty years later. The Protestants remained in full control.

THE SIEGE OF LONDONDERRY

When James II became king in 1685, the situation changed dramatically. James was a Catholic, and he quickly set about restoring Catholic supremacy in Ireland. He appointed a leading Irish Catholic as his lord lieutenant, who put Catholics in power to run the army, the government, and the courts. Many Irish Protestants fled to England or escaped to Holland, where James's daughter Mary and her Protestant husband, William of Orange, lived.

In 1688 seven leading Protestant politicians, who feared that James would reintroduce Catholicism as the state religion, asked William of Orange to take over the British throne. William landed in England in November, and James fled into exile in France. The next month, the Protestant Apprentice Boys of Londonderry, and the people of Enniskillen, shut the gates of their cities to prevent a Catholic army entering and taking over.

> **' ... to rescue the nation and the religion.'**
>
> **Invitation to William of Orange to take over the British throne, 30 June 1688**

In early 1689 James landed in Ireland with an army and advanced on Londonderry. Its 30,000 inhabitants refused to surrender, and James's army began a long siege of the city. The siege ended only when a relief ship finally broke through and brought in supplies. James's army then retreated south, pursued by William's army, which included many Irish and English soldiers as well as

Londonderry was subjected to a bitter siege in 1689.

THE PENAL LAWS

Although the 1691 Treaty of Limerick promised Catholics the same rights they had enjoyed under Charles II, its provisions were ignored. About a million acres of land were confiscated, leaving Catholics with only about one-seventh of the total land. Further laws were passed in the next century by the Protestant-dominated Irish parliament, that further reduced this holding. In 1704 Catholics were forbidden to acquire land from Protestants by marriage or purchase, and their land leases were restricted to 31 years. Catholics were also forbidden to bear arms, own a horse worth more than £5, run schools or send their children abroad for education. Most importantly, they had to take an anti-papal oath before becoming members of parliament, which in effect removed them from parliament. (Protestant dissenters, such as Presbyterians, also faced a religious test that had the same effect.) In 1728 Catholics were forbidden to vote at all. Some of these laws were ignored, but most were enforced rigorously. The laws ensured that all power in Ireland was kept in the hands of members of the Protestant Church of Ireland.

Danish and Swiss, and, of course, Dutch Protestant troops too. (Ironically, James's army also included 3,500 Protestants from Belgium and Germany.)

The two armies finally met on the River Boyne, north of Dublin, on 12 July 1690 (according to the old calendar) - a date still celebrated by Northern Irish Protestants today. James was heavily defeated and again fled into exile. More victories against Catholic troops led to the Treaty of Limerick, which ended the war. Ireland was now under William's control, and the Protestant Ascendancy was complete.

William III, victor at the Battle of the Boyne.

PROTESTANT DOMINATION

1658 Death of Oliver Cromwell

1660 Stuart King Charles II restored

1662 Act of Settlement removes some of the worst aspects of Cromwell's rule

1678 Catholic bishops and priests banned from Ireland

1685 Catholic James II succeeds his brother Charles II and reintroduces Catholics to positions of power

30 June 1688 William of Orange asked to take over British throne

5 Nov 1688 William lands in Torbay, Devon

7 Dec 1688 Apprentice Boys of Londonderry

shut the city gates against Catholic army

25 Dec 1688 James flees into exile, but returns to lead army in Ireland

11 April 1689 William and Mary crowned as joint sovereigns

18 Apr 1689 Fifteen-week siege of Londonderry begins

12 July 1690 William defeats James at the Battle of the Boyne

3 Oct 1691 Treaty of Limerick ends war in Ireland

1704 Popery Act forbids Catholics from acquiring land

1728 Catholics denied the right to vote

A UNITED NATION?

With power secured and the Catholic threat reduced, Protestants felt secure in what was for many of them their new home. They campaigned for greater freedom for Ireland, and a new Protestant nationalism began to flourish.

COLONIAL RULE

Although Irish Protestants controlled both houses of the Irish parliament (the Commons and the Lords), ultimate power still rested with the British government. In reality, Britain governed Ireland like a colony and controlled the Irish economy so that it did not threaten British interests. That hurt Catholics too, because many, unable to own land, had entered trade.

GRATTAN'S PARLIAMENT

In 1775 the brilliant orator Henry Grattan (1746-1820) became an Irish MP. He took advantage of British weakness against the American colonists in their war of independence, and pressed for changes in the relationship between Ireland and the rest of Britain. Grattan knew that Britain used the Catholic threat to keep Ireland divided, and so he pushed through the Catholic Relief Act, which removed the worst of the anti-Catholic land laws of 1704. In 1779 he got rid of most of the anti-Irish trade laws, giving Ireland full control over its trade. He also persuaded the British government to give the Irish parliament the sole right to pass laws for Ireland. Parliamentary and judicial independence from London had finally been secured.

REBELLION

Grattan's success was short-lived. In 1789 the French Revolution began, and its support for equal rights and religious freedom received enthusiastic support in Ireland. In 1791 a young Protestant revolutionary, Theobald Wolfe Tone (1763-98), wrote a pamphlet calling for the repeal of all anti-Catholic penal laws. He co-founded the

> *'I found Ireland on her knees. ... I have traced her progress from injuries to arms, and from arms to liberty. ... Ireland is now a nation.'*
>
> **Henry Grattan in the Irish House of Commons, 16 April 1782**

Irish patriot Theobald Wolfe Tone

THE ORANGE ORDER

The gradual repeal of anti-Catholic land laws caused tension in many areas where Catholic and Protestant tenant farmers competed for land. An increasing rural population added to the tension. In southern Ulster, Protestants set up the 'Peep O'Day Boys' to defend their rights. Catholics set up the 'Defenders'. The two clashed, notably at the Battle of the Diamond in County Armagh in September 1795, when the Defenders were beaten. In 1795 the Protestants reorganised themselves as the Loyal Orange Institution (the Orange Order), named after William of Orange. It soon gained the support of the Protestant gentry and some members of the government, and conducted a violent campaign that drove many Catholics from Ulster. Violence between Orangemen and Catholics led to a temporary ban on the Order in 1825, and a series of Party Procession Acts between 1832-44 stopped provocative marches. These were repealed in 1872, and the Orange Order was confirmed as the main Protestant force in Ireland.

Society of United Irishmen to unite all Irishmen behind radical reform. Two Catholic Relief Acts met many of their demands, but Catholics could still not stand for parliament. Fearful of revolutionary fervour in Ireland, the British government forbade all public meetings and outlawed the United Irishmen. Tone began to plan a full-scale rebellion. In 1798 about 50,000 Irish rose in revolt, but they were eventually crushed by superior British forces. Wolfe Tone's dream of a united Irish republic of Protestants and Catholics was over.

Robert Emmet (1778-1803) was executed in 1803 for his part in a United Irish uprising in Dublin.

ONE IRELAND?

1775 Henry Grattan becomes an Irish MP

1778 Catholic Relief Act passed

1778 The Volunteers set up and lead campaign against British government

1779 Irish parliament gains full control over economy

1782 Catholic Relief Act allows Catholics to buy land

1782 Volunteers press for legislative independence from London; British government grants parliamentary independence to Ireland

1789 French Revolution begins

1791 Wolfe Tone helps found Society of United Irishmen

1792 Catholic Relief Act removes restrictions on Catholic education

1793 Final Relief Act allows Catholics to vote in elections

1794 United Irishmen outlawed

1795 Loyal Orange Institution (the Orange Order) founded

1796 United Irishmen begin to plan revolt

1798 Martial law proclaimed in Ireland; United Irishmen rise in revolt but are easily suppressed

1803 Doomed United Irish rebellion of Robert Emmet in Dublin

IRISH UNION

The United Irishmen's defeat was the last time religion took second place to nationalism in Irish affairs. From then on, Protestant and Catholic interests had little common ground.

UNION

In 1798 the British Prime Minister William Pitt (1759-1806) feared that Ireland could break away if the war against France went badly. He proposed a legislative union of Britain and Ireland, which would end the independence of the Irish parliament. Catholics and Presbyterians were largely in favour because their interests were not represented in the Protestant-dominated Irish parliament, which had long discriminated against them. Protestants who opposed union were bought off with peerages, pensions and other bribes.

The Irish parliament first met to debate the issue in January 1800. One year later the United Kingdom of Great Britain and Ireland was born - although the Irish government was still run from Dublin by the same group of Protestants as before. Catholics could vote for the new parliament but they could not sit in it, despite promises to the contrary by Pitt, and so they soon turned against it. Protestants were increasingly identified with the union, and Catholics against it.

DIVERGENCE

Now the battle lines of Irish politics up to the present day were in place. Led by Daniel O'Connell (1775-1847), Catholics began a mass campaign for emancipation, which the British government grudgingly granted in 1829. O'Connell then began to campaign for Irish Home Rule - the return of an independent parliament - and other reforms, but he failed to get the 1800 Act

Daniel O'Connell led the campaign for Catholic emancipation. He became known as 'The Liberator'.

repealed. O'Connell was a moderate Catholic who believed in constitutional reform within the United Kingdom. His successors - the Young Ireland movement and later the Fenians - were Irish republicans who wanted independence from Britain and were prepared to use violence to achieve it. In Ulster, the last remaining restrictions on Presbyterians - similar to those that had kept Catholics out of public life - were repealed.

THE FAMINE

In 1845 the potato crop – the staple diet of most Irish peasants – was infected by blight, and failed. It failed again in 1846, and then in 1848 and 1849. The British government took some action by importing corn from the USA and setting up relief distribution of food. But its approach was always too little, too late, and relied on landlords to feed those suffering. As a result, the population of Ireland fell from about 8,200,000 – Ireland was one of the most densely populated countries in Europe – to well under six million. About one million died of disease and starvation, and another 1.5 million emigrated, mainly to the USA. The famine reduced the number of small farms - those under five acres - by two-thirds, and drove even more peasants off the land into the cities, or to emigration abroad. It also led to a massive increase in anti-English feeling, which had major political results over the next half-century.

This 19th-century engraving shows Irish peasants digging for potatoes.

Protestants of both sorts - Church of Ireland and Presbyterian - became firm supporters of the union, and Catholics turned firmly against it. Rural battles between Orangemen and Catholics were a regular occurrence, and sectarian riots divided Belfast.

Unlike the rest of Ireland, however, Ulster was becoming increasingly industrialised, with thriving linen, shipbuilding and engineering industries. Wealthy Protestant industrialists now had very little in common with the rural Catholic poor of southern Ireland.

THE UNION AND AFTER

1789 French Revolution begins

1793 Britain at war with France until 1815

1800 Irish parliament accepts the Act of Union with Britain

1801 The United Kingdom of Great Britain and Ireland comes into existence on 1 January – 100 Irish MPs and 32 Irish lords now sit in the British parliament

1823 O'Connell campaigns for emancipation

1828 O'Connell wins Co. Clare by-election but cannot sit in parliament

1829 Catholic Emancipation Act

1840 Municipal Corporation Act: O'Connell first Catholic Lord Mayor of Dublin in 150 years

1840 O'Connell forms National Repeal Association to repeal the Act of Union

1842 Young Ireland movement founded by Protestant and Catholic nationalists committed to cause of Irish independence

1845-48 Irish famine

1848 Young Irish rebellion ends in failure

1849 About 30 Catholics killed when they attack an Orange procession at Dolly's Brae, County Down

HOME RULE?

Ireland dominated British politics throughout the second half of the 19th century. Most Irish people used constitutional means to achieve their ends, but some extreme groups resorted to violence.

LAND AND VOTES

One effect of the famine was to increase the number of tenants evicted from their land for non-payment of rent - there were 16,000 such families in 1849 alone. Tenant societies sprang up across Ireland to defend tenants' rights and campaign for lower rents and more secure tenure. A national tenant league was set up, which promoted an independent Irish Party in parliament to fight its cause. When this alliance collapsed due to lack of support, some turned to violence.

THE FENIANS

The Irish Republican Brotherhood or Fenians - named after a legendary Irish warrior-band, Na Fianna - was a secret society. It was formed in 1858 by former members of Young Ireland 'to make Ireland an independent democratic republic'. There were Fenian uprisings in seven Irish cities in 1867, and public opinion turned in their favour when the leaders were sentenced to long prison terms, or executed. Fenian violence forced the British government to attempt to confront Irish issues.

GLADSTONE'S CONVERSION

The politician most involved with the 'Irish question' was William Gladstone (1809-98), the Liberal prime minister. He disestablished the Irish Church - only 700,000 out of 5.75 million Irish were members - and introduced a series of land acts designed to address tenant grievances.

When Charles Stewart Parnell was elected to parliament at the head of a large contingent of pro-Home Rule Irish MPs, Ireland was firmly in the news. Gladstone could not avoid Home Rule for long.

William Gladstone served four terms as prime minister between 1868 and 1894.

In 1885 Parnell seized an opportunity to bring down Gladstone, and support a Conservative government instead. After a general election, Parnell held the balance of power. But the Conservatives failed to introduce Home Rule, and so Parnell changed sides again, to support a Liberal

PARNELL AND HOME RULE

Like many Irish leaders, Charles Stewart Parnell (1846-91) was Protestant. He was elected to parliament for Meath in 1875 (later for Cork City) and quickly took over the leadership of the Irish Party. He favoured using obstructive tactics in the House of Commons to force the British government to concede Home Rule, and turned his group of MPs into the disciplined Irish Nationalist Party. Outside parliament he formed an alliance with the Irish National Land League, set up to campaign for 'the land of Ireland for the people of Ireland'. The league organised popular demonstrations against evictions and shunned those who bought evicted land (notably a landlord's agent, Captain Boycott, whose name soon entered the language). Parnell achieved success in persuading Gladstone to adopt Home Rule, but his own career, and the cause of Home Rule, was wrecked when he was named in a divorce action. His Catholic supporters were outraged by his supposed immorality and Parnell was forced out of public life.

government. By now, Gladstone was convinced Home Rule was the only solution to Irish unrest. He introduced his first Home Rule Bill to parliament in 1886.

Some Liberal MPs agreed with the Conservatives, that Home Rule could not be forced on an unwilling Protestant, unionist population in Ulster. The bill was defeated. Gladstone resigned, but returned to power in 1892 and introduced a second bill. This passed a vote in the Commons, but was defeated in the House of Lords. Home Rule was shelved again.

LAND AND HOME RULE

1850 Tenant League established in Dublin

1858 Irish Republican Brotherhood or Fenians set up in Dublin

1867 Fenian uprisings in Ireland and violent incidents in England

1868 Gladstone first becomes prime minister

1869 Irish Church disestablished

1870 First Land Act passed securing tenure if rent is paid

1874 59 pro-Home Rule Irish MPs returned to Westminster

1875 Charles Stewart Parnell becomes MP for Meath

1877 Parnell takes over leadership of Irish Party

1881 Gladstone's Land Act introduces 'three Fs': fair rents, fixity of tenure, free sale

1882 Irish MPs form Irish Nationalist Party·

Nov 1885 Irish Nationalists win 85 seats and hold balance of power

Dec 1885 Gladstone expresses support for Home Rule

Jan 1886 Nationalists and Liberals bring down Conservatives

June 1886 Home Rule Bill defeated

1890 Parnell named in divorce action

1893 House of Lords reject second Home Rule Bill

1894 Gladstone resigns for final time

THE ULSTER CRISIS

Although Home Rule fell from the political agenda after Gladstone retired, it never went away. When the issue resurfaced in 1912, it brought Britain to the edge of civil war.

KILLING BY KINDNESS

The Conservative governments of 1895-1905 tried to smother Irish nationalism. They improved social conditions, introduced agricultural improvement boards, built roads and railways and set up a local government system in which women could both vote and stand for office. But Home Rule demands did not disappear.

In 1906 a new Liberal government came to power. It was soon engaged in a battle with the Conservative-dominated House of Lords when it tried to get through a radical budget. After two general elections on the issue the Lords gave way, and lost the power to reject legislation for more than two years. An unexpected result of the elections was that the 84 Irish MPs now held the balance of power. They used that power to demand Home Rule for Ireland.

THE HOME RULE CRISIS

The new Home Rule Bill had every chance of becoming law, because the Liberal and Irish MPs had a large majority in the Commons, and the Lords now had no veto. Many Irish Protestants, however, feared Home Rule would bring domination by a Catholic-run government in Dublin. Throughout 1912-13, unionists - led by the Dublin lawyer Sir Edward Carson MP

ULSTER'S RESISTANCE

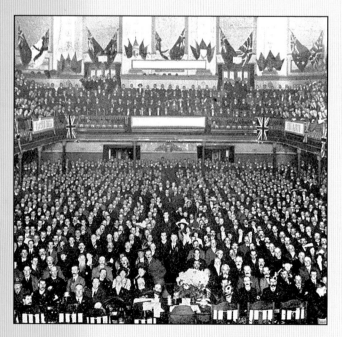

The eve of Covenant day in Belfast City Hall.

Asquith's Liberal government (1908-15) wanted only to consider Home Rule for all 32 counties of Ireland. It did not anticipate the stiff resistance to this from Ulster Protestants of all classes and professions. In 1912, 250,000 unionists signed a Solemn League and Covenant in Belfast City Hall: 'Being convinced ... that Home Rule would be disastrous to the material well-being of Ulster, ... subversive of our civil and religious freedom, destructive of our citizenship, ... [we] hereby pledge ourselves ... in using all means which may be necessary to defeat the present conspiracy to set up a Home Rule parliament.' The unionists received full support from the opposition Conservative Party in the British parliament, led by Andrew Bonar Law (later prime minister). The strength of organised resistance led to the compromise of partition.

(1854-1935) - held huge and increasingly militant rallies in opposition to the bill. They set up the Ulster Volunteer Force (UVF) to resist Home Rule by armed force, and smuggled in arms from Europe.

The British government tried to compromise by excluding the nine Ulster counties from a Home Rule parliament. In response, Irish nationalists set up their own Irish Volunteers to achieve Home Rule for the whole of Ireland. The country was now on the brink of civil war. There were major shipments of guns arriving openly at Irish ports, and British army officers threatened to mutiny if they were ordered to put down a unionist uprising in Ulster.

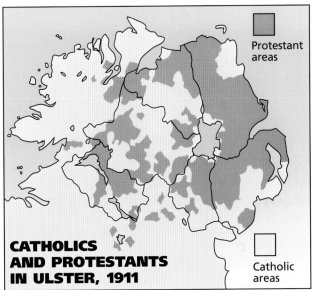

CATHOLICS AND PROTESTANTS IN ULSTER, 1911

Protestant areas

Catholic areas

Ulster Volunteer Force members on parade in 1912.

The situation was explosive, but in June 1914 the heir to the Austrian throne was assassinated in Sarajevo. That began a chain of events leading to the outbreak of World War I, and Ireland had to wait. The British government decided to make Home Rule law, but suspend its effects for the duration of the war. They promised that special provision would be made for Ulster. The partition of Ireland now looked inevitable.

THE ROAD TO WAR

1898 Irish Local Government Act sets up county councils

1903 Wyndham's Land Act encourages sale of whole estates

1905 Ulster Unionist Council unifies various unionist organisations

1906 Liberals win landslide victory in general election

1909 House of Lords defeat Liberal Budget

1911 Parliament Act restricts right of House of Lords to veto bills

April 1912 Home Rule Bill introduced

Sep 1912 Unionists sign covenant against Home Rule

Jan 1913 Unionists set up Ulster Volunteer Force to resist with force if necessary

Nov 1913 Irish nationalists set up Irish Volunteers

April 1914 Massive gun-running by Ulster Volunteers into port of Larne

May 1914 Home Rule Bill passes Commons for third and final time

July 1914 Gun-running by Irish Volunteers intercepted at Howth

Aug 1914 Outbreak of World War I

Sept 1914 Home Rule Bill becomes law but is suspended for the war

THE EASTER RISING

Home Rule was put aside during World War I, but the issue did not go away. In 1916 it exploded in a desperate uprising.

THE REVOLUTION IS PLANNED

When war broke out in 1914, most Irish Volunteers supported the call from John Redmond, the Nationalist Party leader, to volunteer for military service in the British army. A minority refused and, keeping the same name, set up their own organisation. Three officers in the new group - Patrick Pearse, Thomas MacDonagh and Joseph Plunkett - were also members of the secretive and shadowy Irish Republican Brotherhood, whose aim was to win Ireland's freedom through revolution. Along with Volunteer members Eamonn Ceannt, Seán Mac Diarmada and Tom Clarke, and socialist leader James Connolly, who led his own Irish Citizen Army, they planned an uprising against British rule.

EASTER 1916

The uprising on Easter Monday, 24 April 1916, was a disaster. A group of Volunteers seized the General Post Office in Dublin and raised the Irish tricolour - green and orange for nationalist and unionist, with a white band for union in between - while Pearse read out a proclamation from 'the Provisional Government of the Irish Republic to the people of Ireland' signed by the seven leaders. Other buildings were seized, but the rebels received little support and were outnumbered by British forces. They eventually agreed to a ceasefire.

Dublin's General Post Office was badly damaged in the 1916 uprising.

THE AFTERMATH

The rising had little impact outside Dublin, and many in the city were horrified at the damage done by the rebels to their beautiful Georgian buildings. But when the British executed 15 republican leaders and interned 2,000 more, convicting 170 by courts martial, public opinion turned in favour of the republican cause.

> 'We hereby proclaim the Irish Republic as a Sovereign Independent State, and we pledge our lives and the lives of our comrades in arms to the cause of its freedom, of its welfare and of its exaltation among the nations.'
>
> 1916 declaration of the Irish Republic

SINN FÉIN

At the end of the 19th century, attempts were made to revive the Gaelic language and promote Irish culture and history. Gaelic sport and language associations were set up, many of them dominated by Irish Republican Brotherhood members. The political focus of this movement was Sinn Féin, established by Arthur Griffith (1871-1922) in 1905. Sinn Féin is a Gaelic phrase meaning 'We ourselves' or 'Ourselves alone' and was coined, ironically, by a cousin of the Unionist leader, Sir Edward Carson. The organisation wanted to re-establish the full political, economic and cultural independence of Ireland from Britain through a policy of non-co-operation, including a boycott of parliament. Although Sinn Féin played no part in the Easter Rising, it soon took over leadership of the republican movement. Both the Irish Volunteers and the Irish Republican Brotherhood came under its wing in October 1917. Now led by Eamon de Valera, it stated that: 'Sinn Féin aims at securing the international recognition of Ireland as an independent Irish Republic.' On that policy, it fought and won a massive victory in Ireland in the general election of 1918.

The main casualty of the Easter Rising was the Irish Nationalist Party, for their parliamentary approach now seemed irrelevant. The main beneficiary was Sinn Féin (see box at right). In February 1917 Count Plunkett, father of one of the 1916 leaders, stood in a by-election for Sinn Féin and won an easy victory against a Nationalist candidate. He then refused to take his seat at Westminster. Five other Sinn Féin candidates won by-elections, notably Eamon de Valera (1882-1975), one of the main leaders in 1916. All refused to take their seats. As the British continued to suppress republican dissent, support for Sinn Féin rose. At the end of the war, a general election was held. Sinn Féin swept the board in Ireland with 73 seats - including the first woman elected as an MP, Countess Markievicz - while the Irish Nationalists held only 6, and the Unionists 26 seats.

THE IRISH REVOLUTION			
1905 Arthur Griffith forms Sinn Féin	**April 1916** Easter Rising in Dublin: 450 are killed, 318 of them republicans and innocent civilians	**Feb 1917** Count Plunkett wins Roscommon North by-election	**May 1918** Sinn Féin leaders arrested and party banned
Aug 1914 170,000 Irish Volunteers volunteer for the British army effort; 10,000 set up own organisation	**May 1916** 15 rebel leaders executed, including Plunkett, Pearse and Connolly	**July 1917** Eamon de Valera wins Clare, East by-election for Sinn Féin	**Dec 1918** Sinn Féin wins 73 Irish seats in general election (47% of total vote) but it does not contest four out of of six Nationalist seats for fear of splitting the vote
May 1915 IRB plans the Easter Rising	**Dec 1916** Many republican internees are freed, boosting their cause at home	**Oct 1917** Sinn Féin assumes leadership of the Irish republican movement	

PARTITION

The general election of December 1918 was a watershed in Irish politics. It led to the partition of the island, and the establishment of Northern Ireland as a separate state.

THE DÁIL

The 73 elected Sinn Féin MPs refused to go to Westminster, and instead formed a 'Dáil Eireann' (Assembly of Ireland) to run the country. This declared Irish independence and set up a republican government. It even appointed delegates to the Versailles Peace Conference that followed World War I, hoping to gain international recognition for the new republic. It also established a parallel legal, financial and local government structure to run Ireland instead of the British.

None of this was recognised by the British government, which used armed force to suppress the republican government. Nor was it recognised by the six Nationalist and 26 Unionist MPs - all but four from Ulster - who refused to take part.

PARTITION

The solution chosen by the British government was the partition of Ireland. The 1920 Government of Ireland Act established two Home Rule parliaments. One, in Dublin, represented 26 of the 32 Irish counties; the other, in Belfast, represented the six Ulster counties - Antrim, Armagh, Londonderry, Down, Fermanagh and Tyrone - where opposition to all-Ireland Home Rule was strongest.

Sinn Féin leaders at the first Dáil Eireann, 21 January 1919. In the front row, second from left, is Michael Collins. Eamon de Valera is in the front row, fifth from left.

DIVIDED ULSTER, 1920

LONDONDERRY
DONEGAL
ANTRIM
TYRONE
DOWN
FERMANAGH
ARMAGH
MONAGHAN
CAVAN

IRISH SEA

■ Catholic majority

■ Protestant majority Dotted line = new Northern Ireland border

The two parliaments had limited powers, and were linked by an all-embracing Council of Ireland. For unionists, however, this solution presented a problem: it broke the union of an Ireland united with Britain, and introduced a measure of Home Rule that they had always resisted. Most, however, reluctantly accepted Home Rule for Northern Ireland (as it now became known) as the best way of retaining a link with the rest of Britain.

THE SOUTH

Republicans refused to accept partition. They fought a bloody war of independence against the British until the formation of the Irish Free State was conceded. This was an independent dominion, like Canada, within the British Empire. Those who opposed this settlement then fought a civil war against the Free State that ended after many deaths in 1923. From then on, the history of northern and southern Ireland diverges, only coming together again half a century later when the Troubles began.

THE BIRTH OF THE IRA

The first clash between the British and Irish after the 1918 general election occurred on the day that the Dáil first met: 21 January 1919. A group of Irish Volunteers killed two members of the Royal Irish Constabulary, who were escorting explosives to a quarry in Co. Tipperary. The Irish Volunteers had been under Sinn Féin control since 1917 and had trained, armed and organised themselves to exert pressure on Britain to recognise the Irish Republic they had declared at Easter 1916. Now that a republican government was established in Dublin, they acted on its behalf and renamed themselves the Irish Republican Army. Using guerrilla tactics, they waged a successful and bloody war against the British. A truce was finally declared in July 1921.

SOUTHERN IRELAND

Jan 1919 Sinn Féin MPs set up Dáil in Dublin to run Ireland

April 1919 De Valera elected president of the Dáil

Jan 1920 British recruit former soldiers to reinforce Royal Irish Constabulary; they commit appalling atrocities against suspected IRA members

Dec 1920 Government of Ireland Act partitions Ireland

July 1921 Truce between IRA and British army

Dec 1921 Anglo-Irish Treaty signed setting up Irish Free State

June 1922 Anti-Treaty IRA forces in Dublin attacked by Free State troops; civil war starts

April 1923 End of Irish civil war

1926 De Valera founds new party, Fianna Fáil, and re-enters Dáil

1932 De Valera elected prime minister

1937 New constitution establishes Eire

1939-45 Eire stays neutral in World War Two

1949 Eire becomes the Republic of Ireland and leaves Commonwealth

1973 Republic of Ireland and Britain (including Northern Ireland) join European Community

STORMONT

On 22 June 1921 King George V opened the new Northern Irish parliament in Belfast City Hall. He appealed for peace and reconciliation in Ireland, but those hopes were not achieved.

SETTING THE BOUNDARIES

The new Northern Irish state faced many problems. Its boundaries were artificial, based on old county borders, so Protestants in three of the nine Ulster counties found themselves citizens of a Catholic state to which they had no loyalty. Many Catholics now formed a minority in a Protestant state. The Anglo-Irish Treaty set up a boundary commission to adjust the frontier between south and north. Even though one-third of people in Northern Ireland were Catholic (in the 1911 census they had formed a majority in Fermanagh, Tyrone, Armagh, southern Down, Londonderry and parts of Belfast) the existing border was confirmed.

At first both communities waged sectarian violence against the other. After the Free State was set up in early 1922, Protestants intimidated and attacked Catholics as internal enemies of Northern Ireland, and 232 Catholics were killed, 11,000 made jobless, and 23,000 made homeless. More than 4,500 Catholic-owned shops and businesses were burnt or looted, and £3m of their property was destroyed. Thousands of refugees fled south across the border. To protect the new state, the Northern Irish government took special powers and set up the Protestant-dominated, semi-military Royal Ulster Constabulary, supported by armed B-Special Reserves.

A PROTESTANT STATE

Unionists used their control of the Northern Irish parliament (after 1932 this was known as Stormont after its new meeting place)

The Northern Irish parliament met at Stormont, shown above, from 1932.

Sir James Craig (1871-1940), first Ulster Unionist prime minister of Northern Ireland.

KEEPING CATHOLICS OUT

Ulster Unionists achieved domination by rigging local government borders, that is, by altering them to their own advantage. The worst example was Londonderry, where three-fifths of the population were Catholic and two-fifths Protestant. The borders of its three wards were drawn so that North Ward, with 5,000 Protestant voters, returned eight unionist councillors and Waterside Ward, again with 5,000 Protestants, returned four unionists, while South Ward, with 15,000 Catholics, returned only eight nationalists, giving 10,000 Protestants a majority of four seats on the local council over 15,000 nationalists. New houses for Catholics were packed into South Ward and the city boundaries were restricted to keep some Catholic estates out of the city altogether. In total, about one-fifth of all Catholic voters in the province lived in these altered wards. Proportional representation was abolished to weaken minor (usually nationalist) parties, and only ratepayers could vote in local elections – a practice that discriminated against Catholics.

and also their control of local government to discriminate against Catholics. Civil service posts, local government jobs and housing were offered to Protestants, but not to Catholics. Protestant businesses refused to employ Catholics, and Protestant politicians set up new industries in Protestant areas.

This situation continued for 50 years. As recently as 1966, only one of the nine commission members appointed to oversee the construction of the new town of Craigavon was Catholic, despite the benefits the town would bring to Catholics. In 1972 only seven of the 75 school bus drivers in Catholic-majority County Fermanagh were Catholic, and 97.5% of all Belfast City Corporation jobs were held by Protestants, although Catholics made up more than one-quarter of the city's entire population.

NORTHERN IRELAND

Dec 1920 Government of Ireland Act partitions Ireland

Feb 1921 Sir James Craig becomes first prime minister of Northern Ireland

June 1921 King George V opens new parliament in Belfast

April 1922 Special Powers Act gives extensive powers to security forces, including detention without trial

Summer 1922 Sectarian rioting in Belfast leaves 232 Catholics dead

Sept 1922 Proportional representation abolished for local elections

1929 Proportional representation abolished for parliamentary elections

1932 New parliament buildings at Stormont opened

1935 Sectarian rioting breaks out again in Belfast

1949 British government recognises new Republic of Ireland and guarantees that status of Northern Ireland would remain unchanged unless its parliament decided otherwise

THE CIVIL RIGHTS MOVEMENT

During the 1960s, reforms removed the most blatant forms of discrimination against Catholics. Pressure from the new civil rights movement, however, led to increased violence.

MODERATE REFORMS

In the 1960s moderate unionists realised that they must address Catholic concerns, or perhaps lose control of Northern Ireland. The rising Catholic birthrate and the growing success of the non-sectarian Northern Ireland Labour Party threatened to capture Belfast from Unionist control.

The new Unionist prime minister, Terence O'Neill (1914-90), introduced reforms designed to remove the worst excesses of the old system. He even met the Irish taoiseach (prime minister) for the first time since the two states were created in the 1920s. In 1967 the Northern Ireland Civil Rights Association (NICRA) was formed. It drew ideas from the non-violent civil rights movement of Martin Luther King in the USA. It was non-sectarian, stressing 'British rights for British citizens' and 'one man, one vote' rather than raising exclusively Catholic concerns. At first, NICRA demonstrations were peaceful, but on 5 October 1968 a civil rights march in Londonderry was attacked by baton-wielding officers of the Royal Ulster Constabulary (RUC). Two nights of rioting in the Catholic Bogside area followed.

The British government forced O'Neill to make more radical reforms, but civil rights demonstrators were now met by loyalist counter-demonstrations - often organised by the Presbyterian cleric, the Rev Ian Paisley (1926-). On 4 January 1969 a civil-rights march from Belfast to Londonderry

Led by helmet-wearing police, Ulster Volunteers and Protestant sympathisers march in Londonderry on 4 January 1969, leading to violent clashes with civil-rights protesters.

Since the 1960s, Ian Paisley has been the face of hardline Unionism, rejecting all compromise.

THE REBIRTH OF THE IRA

After the partition of Ireland and its defeat in the Irish Civil War of 1922-23, the Irish Republican Army lost support. It was banned by the Irish government in 1936. Bombing campaigns against Britain in 1939-40 and in Northern Ireland in 1956-62 both failed, because of lack of nationalist support. When violence erupted in Northern Ireland in August 1969, the IRA was so ineffectual that graffiti appeared on Belfast walls stating 'IRA – I Ran Away'. Many in the organisation preferred to pursue a radical socialist agenda rather than a traditional republican one, so some militants in Belfast broke away and set up the Provisional IRA. They were supported by traditional republicans in the south in organising and arming Catholic resistance to the British. The 'official' IRA, meanwhile, took little part in the violence and declared a ceasefire in 1972, renouncing violence the next year.

was viciously attacked by a loyalist mob, including several off-duty members of the B-Specials. Rioting broke out across the province, as it did again repeatedly throughout the summer. On 12 August 1969, following a Protestant Apprentice Boys march in Londonerry, loyalists attacked the Bogside for three days. Catholics fought back with petrol bombs, and the RUC used CS (tear) gas. On the afternoon of 14 August, the RUC commander asked for British army help, and the first troops were on the streets by 5 pm. By now, many Protestants believed a nationalist uprising was underway and attacked Catholic districts of Belfast. On 15 August the army entered the Falls Road district for the first time.

THE ROAD TO VIOLENCE

1963 Terence O'Neill becomes prime minister

1965 O'Neill meets taoiseach of the Irish Republic

1967 Northern Ireland Civil Rights Association (NICRA) founded

1967–68 O'Neill meets new Irish taoiseach

Oct 1968 First violent confrontation between NICRA and the RUC

Nov 1968 British prime minister demands reforms

Nov 1968 Loyalists occupy Armagh city centre to prevent a civil-rights meeting

Jan 1969 NICRA 'long march' from Belfast to Derry attacked by loyalists supported by some RUC and B-Special officers

April 1969 Bernadette Devlin – an independent republican and civil rights supporter – wins Mid-Ulster by-election for the Westminster parliament

Aug 1969 Widespread rioting in Derry and then Belfast leads to British army deployment on the streets of both cities

Sept 1969 Militants take over Belfast IRA

Jan 1970 Provisional IRA splits from the 'official' IRA

THE TROUBLES

The presence of the British army in Northern Ireland was meant to stop the violence, and bring peace back to the streets. In fact, it had the opposite effect.

THE ARMY'S ROLE

When the army first arrived in Londonderry and Belfast, the Catholic population welcomed the troops as protectors against Protestant attacks, which continued. Between August 1969 and February 1973, 60,000 people in Belfast - about 10 per cent of the population - had been forced from their homes by sectarian violence and intimidation; 80 per cent of them were Catholics.

But the army soon lost Catholic support. Troops raided their houses and stopped cars to look for hidden weapons - 17,000 homes were searched in 1971 and 250,000 more

> **'We've no doubt that military victory is within our grasp.'**
>
> **Sean MacStiofain, Provisional IRA chief of staff, early 1972**

THE IRA'S CLAIM TO LEGITIMACY

The IRA saw itself as the army of the Irish Republic, established after the 1918 general election by Sinn Féin. They refused to accept partition and the establishment of the Free State, believing that both compromised the sovereignty of a 32-county Republic of Ireland. The IRA official manual states that the IRA 'is the direct representative of the 1918 Dáil Eireann parliament, and that as such they are the legal and lawful government of the Irish Republic, which has the moral right to pass laws for, and to claim jurisdiction over ... all of its people regardless of creed or loyalty.' The IRA (and its political wing, Sinn Féin) considered it had the right to fight the British, remove them from Ireland and so reunify Ireland as one country.

over the next five years, while four million vehicles were stopped in the year from April 1973. Catholics came to see the British army as an occupying force working for the Protestant-dominated Northern Irish government. Many turned to the IRA for help.

During 1971 the IRA went on the offensive. They shot British soldiers, bombed commercial targets and enforced strict discipline in Catholic areas by punishing criminals and those who disobeyed IRA rules. The army responded in turn by treating Catholic areas as IRA strongholds. They imposed curfews, raided houses and stopped and searched people. These tactics increased Catholic mistrust of British rule and increased IRA support.

BLOODY SUNDAY

In August 1971 the Northern Irish government introduced internment - the imprisonment of suspects without trial. They arrested 342 republicans. The result was a massive upsurge in violence, with 30 soldiers, 11 police officers and 73 civilians killed. Some 7,000 people, mainly Catholics, fled their homes in fear and despair.

On 30 January 1972 the British army's Parachute Regiment shot dead 13 unarmed demonstrators in Londonderry. That day, and the deaths that shocked the world, has become known as Bloody Sunday.

Violence escalated across Northern Ireland in protest, and civil war was again a real possibility. In response, the British government suspended the Northern Irish

Londonderry demonstrators try to reach safety as soldiers open fire on Bloody Sunday, 30 January 1972, killing 13 people.

parliament and imposed direct rule from Westminster. The IRA claimed this as a major victory and declared a seven-day ceasefire, holding discussions with the British government. When these failed to achieve peace, the IRA returned to war.

THE TROUBLES

August 1969 Violence erupts across Northern Ireland

Jan 1970 Provisional IRA splits from the 'official' IRA

Feb 1971 First British soldier killed by IRA

Mar 1971 Unionist prime minister James

Chichester-Clark resigns complaining that Britain was not sending enough troops to the province; replaced by hardliner Brian Faulkner

9 Aug 1971 Internment of republican suspects begins

1972 Bloody Sunday – 13 killed by British army in Londonderry

Mar 1972 Stormont parliament suspended and direct rule imposed from London

June 1972 IRA ceasefire

July 1972 IRA holds secret talks with the British government

21 July 1972 IRA detonates 22 bombs in Belfast in one hour: nine killed

Dec 1975 Internment ends: in total, 1,981 people were detained (1,874 republicans, 107 loyalists)

THE LONG WAR

After the imposition of direct rule, the British government tried a number of ways to solve the political problems of Northern Ireland and end the conflict. None of them worked for long.

SUNNINGDALE

Increasing attacks by the IRA, and the collapse of Home Rule, led many Protestants to fear betrayal by Britain. Loyalist paramilitary groups adopted the IRA's tactics and attacked Catholics - 80 were killed in 1972 alone - to show that loyalists would fight if Britain abandoned them to a united Ireland. As the gap between the two warring sides widened, the British government struggled to find a political solution acceptable to all.

In 1973 the government proposed the return of devolved government, provided that power was shared between unionist

> ### 'Dublin is just a Sunningdale away'
>
> **Political slogan of the three-party anti-Sunningdale United Ulster Unionist Council during the February 1974 Westminster elections**

and nationalist parties. After elections, the three main constitutional parties - the Ulster Unionist Party (UUP), Social Democratic & Labour Party (SDLP) and the moderate Alliance Party - formed an executive. The new executive met representatives of the British and Irish

THE ANGLO-IRISH AGREEMENT

By 1980 both the British and Irish governments felt that disagreements about Northern Ireland were damaging both countries. They urgently looked for ways to move towards peace. The British and Irish prime ministers set up an council to examine their relationships. After months of discussions, they published the Anglo-Irish Agreement in 1985. The British recognised the right of Ireland to be consulted and make proposals concerning the future of Northern Ireland, while the Irish agreed that a united Ireland could only come about by Northern Irish consent. The agreement was a huge advance for constitutional nationalists, as Ireland was now officially involved in Northern Irish affairs.

Irish Prime Minister Garret FitzGerald (left) and British Prime Minister Margaret Thatcher sign the Agreement on 15 November 1985.

governments at Sunningdale, in Berkshire. They planned to set up a Council of Ireland, the first three-government meeting since 1925. The involvement of the Irish Republic in Northern Irish affairs led to massive unionist protests. A general strike brought power-sharing to an end.

DIRECT RULE AGAIN

After the re-imposition of direct rule, sectarian murders and terrorist violence continued on both sides. The IRA conducted a bombing campaign on the British mainland. Various constitutional settlements were tried, but all failed. The British government increased security measures, trying to limit the conflict.

HUNGER STRIKES

This situation changed in 1981 when IRA members in the Maze (formerly Long Kesh) prison went on hunger strike, demanding recognition as political prisoners. The British government refused to give them that status, but the prisoners won international attention. One of them, Bobby Sands, was elected an MP, and died one month later. Two more hunger strikers were elected to the Dáil in Dublin. Although the strike was later called off, and the British government

made concessions, the main effect of the strike was to encourage Sinn Féin to re-enter electoral politics. They hoped to replace the SDLP as the main nationalist and republican party in the north.

MP-elect Bobby Sands, who died while on hunger strike in 1981.

OPPOSING SIDES

1966 Paramilitary Ulster Volunteer Force formed	**Oct 1971** Ian Paisley forms loyalist Democratic Unionist Party (DUP)	**May 1974** Ulster Workers' Council strike brings down assembly	**Spring 1981** Bobby Sands dies in May after 66 days on hunger strike
Apr 1970 Alliance Party of Northern Ireland (APNI) formed	**Mar 1973** British government proposals for power-sharing	**Nov 1974** 19 killed and 252 wounded by IRA bomb in Birmingham	**Autumn 1981** Sinn Féin re-enters electoral politics
Aug 1970 Social Democratic and Labour Party (SDLP) formed	**Nov 1973** Devolved assembly meets	**May 1980** Anglo–Irish Intergovernmental Council	**Oct 1984** IRA bomb Brighton hotel where Conservative Party is meeting
Sept 1971 Loyalist paramilitary group the Ulster Defence Association formed	**Dec 1973** Northern Irish, British and Irish governments set up Council of Ireland	**Mar 1981** Hunger strike launched by IRA prisoners in the Maze (Long Kesh)	**Nov 1985** Anglo–Irish Agreement signed

THE ROAD TO PEACE

The Anglo-Irish Agreement of 1985 marked a watershed in Northern Irish politics. It paved the way for a potentially lasting peace in the province.

THE POLITICAL FALLOUT

The Anglo-Irish Agreement gave hope to nationalists and republicans that their views were being taken into account. They believed that a future reunification of the island might be possible. Unionists, who had relied on a strategy of 'masterful inactivity' to defend their position in the United Kingdom, saw the agreement as a joint British-Irish threat to their future. They protested strongly, but the British government ignored them. Unionists had to rethink their approach. Some wanted integration with Britain, or the return of some form of Home Rule. A few even wanted outright independence.

SINN FÉIN'S ROLE

Although IRA - and loyalist - violence continued, members of Sinn Féin (the IRA's political wing) used both the ballot box and the gun to achieve success. By the late 1980s, however, Sinn Féin had less than 10 per cent support in Northern Ireland (1.2 per cent in the Republic), while the SDLP's support was over twice that. Sinn Féin then began to work with the SDLP, hoping to overtake it.

The SDLP leader, John Hume (1937-) held secret discussions with Sinn Féin leader, Gerry Adams (1948-). The British government encouraged this. In 1991 it said that Britain had no 'selfish, strategic or

Key players in Northern Ireland politics: Gerry Adams, Sinn Féin (far left) John Hume, SDLP (second from left) and David Trimble, UUP (far right) pose with US President Bill Clinton in 1992.

MAKING THE PEACE

The discussions that took place after the paramilitary ceasefires of 1994 were complex and confusing. Nationalists wanted recognition of the Irish identity of northern Catholics. Unionists feared the new SDLP/Sinn Féin alliance, and pressed the IRA for a complete decommissioning of all weapons before they would talk to Sinn Féin. The British government placated both sides and, with the Irish government, issued a joint declaration in November 1995. This proposed exploratory talks amongst all parties, including Sinn Féin, alongside talks about decommissioning all paramilitary weapons. An international body, chaired by former US senator George Mitchell, would advise on decommissioning. A massive IRA bomb attack in London kept Sinn Féin excluded, but eventually the process began with elections to a Forum of Peace and Reconciliation. When the IRA resumed its ceasefire, Sinn Féin could enter the talks at last.

economic interest in Northern Ireland'. By 1993 the two nationalist leaders reached agreement. Then the Irish and British governments agreed 'to foster agreement and reconciliation, leading to a new political framework within Northern Ireland, for the whole island and within these islands'. US President Bill Clinton supported this approach.

CEASEFIRES

With both governments and both nationalist parties now moving in the same direction, the IRA announced a 'complete and unequivocal' ceasefire. Six weeks later, loyalist paramilitary groups did the same. Faced with this widespread outbreak of peace, Unionists began to consider power-sharing once again. They were encouraged to do so because such arrangements were already in place in almost half the 26 local authorities.

A recurring source of tension in Northern Ireland is the summer 'Marching Season', when Orange Order parades, such as this one, take place.

ROAD TO PEACE

1983 Gerry Adams president of Sinn Féin

Nov 1985 Anglo–Irish Agreement signed

Jan 1986 All 15 Unionist MPs at Westminster resign their seats

Nov 1987 IRA bombs a Remembrance Day service in Enniskillen, killing 11 Protestants

1989 Sinn Féin begins political dialogue with SDLP

Aug 1993 SDLP and Sinn Féin leaders issue joint statement

Dec 1993 British and Irish prime ministers agree Downing Street Declaration to work together for peace

Aug 1994 IRA announces 'complete and unequivocal' ceasefire

Oct 1994 Loyalist paramilitaries announce ceasefire

Feb 1995 British and Irish governments recognise Ireland's role in Northern Ireland

Jan 1996 Mitchell Commission starts work

Jun 1996 Peace talks open without Sinn Féin, excluded because of IRA violence

July 1997 IRA resumes ceasefire

Sept 1997 Sinn Féin enters peace talks for first time

THE GOOD FRIDAY AGREEMENT

The peace agreement signed at 5 pm on 10 April 1998 – Good Friday – represents, to many people, the best hope of a lasting peace in Northern Ireland.

REACHING A DEAL

When Sinn Féin joined the peace talks in September 1997, Ian Paisley's hardline Democratic Unionist Party walked out. The negotiations were dominated by the UUP of David Trimble (1944-) and the SDLP of John Hume, supported by British Prime Minister Tony Blair and Irish Taoiseach Bertie Ahern, with US President Bill Clinton in the background. George Mitchell, who chaired the meeting, set a deadline of Thursday 9 April 1998, but in fact the talks ran on into the next day. Mr Trimble was unable to get all his colleagues to agree, but all the parties did sign the agreement.

THE AGREEMENT

The Belfast, or Good Friday, Agreement is a complex document. As a matter of principle, it confirmed that any change in the status of Northern Ireland could only come about with the consent of the majority in the province.

The agreement set up a devolved 108-member assembly, elected by proportional representation. All legislation must be agreed by a majority of members from both communities. The leader of the biggest party heads an executive as first minister, with the second party's leader as his or her deputy. Ten ministers, elected proportionally from all parties, are each responsible for a department, such as housing. The ministers do not have to agree with each other as they would have to do in traditional cabinet government.

> *'All I can say is that I'll not be changing. I will go to the grave with the convictions I have.'*
>
> **Ian Paisley, in an interview for a BBC programme in 1999**

Mo Mowlam was Secretary of State for Northern Ireland at the time of the Good Friday Agreement.

AGREEING THE AGREEMENT

The Agreement was put to the vote on both sides of the border. In the Republic, 95% of voters approved it; in Northern Ireland, 71.1%, including a majority of unionists, were in favour. In elections to the assembly the next month, 75.5% voted for candidates in favour of the agreement, giving them 80 seats to 28 against. The SDLP emerged as winner with 22% of the votes and 24 seats, but the UUP's 28 seats made David Trimble first minister with the SDLP's Seamus Mallon his deputy. The anti-agreement DUP got 20 seats, Sinn Féin 18, the Alliance Party 6 and others 12. The IRA remained on ceasefire, but some members broke away and formed the Continuity and Real IRAs. The latter set off a car bomb in Omagh that killed 29, the largest single atrocity of the Troubles. All parties, however, worked hard to make the Agreement stick, including the IRA.

The aftermath of the Omagh bomb on 19 August 1998, which killed 29 people.

Some issues, like law and order, remain under British control. Three other organisations were set up: a North-South Council drawn from delegates from both sides of the Irish border responsible for cross-border issues; a British-Irish Intergovernmental Conference to deal with relations between the two national governments; and a British-Irish Council with representatives of the other devolved governments of Britain (Scotland and Wales) together with Northern Ireland and the Irish Republic.

The Royal Ulster Constabulary was reformed; the Patten Commission renamed it the Police Service of Northern Ireland in 1998. A new badge carried symbols 'entirely free from any association with British or Irish states'. Importantly, an Independent International Commission on Decommissioning under a Canadian general, John de Chasterlain, oversaw the decommissioning of all paramilitary weapons. Paramilitary - including IRA - prisoners whose groups observed the ceasefire were released in two years.

GOOD FRIDAY

Sept 1995 David Trimble leader of UUP

Jun 1996 Peace talks open without Sinn Féin, excluded because of IRA violence

May 1997 Tony Blair's Labour Party wins landslide election victory in British general election

June 1997 Bertie Ahern becomes Irish taoiseach

July 1997 IRA resume ceasefire

Sept 1997 Sinn Féin enters peace talks for first time

April 1998 Good Friday Agreement signed

May 1998 Voters in both parts of Ireland overwhelmingly support agreement

June 1998 First elections to devolved assembly

Aug 1998 Real IRA set off car bomb in Omagh

Oct 1998 Trimble and Hume jointly win Nobel Peace Prize

May 2000 IRA promise to 'initiate a process that will completely and verifiably put IRA arms beyond use'

NORTHERN IRELAND TODAY

Despite the initial success of the Good Friday Agreement, Northern Ireland is still not fully at peace. Its leading politicians seem as far apart as ever.

A TROUBLED EXISTENCE

After the assembly elections in June 1998, power was due to be transferred to the new executive in March 1999. For devolved government to work, however, all sides have to trust each other and work together. This degree of trust does not yet exist, largely because the Unionists do not trust Sinn Féin and do not believe that the IRA is ready to disarm completely. The assembly and executive have been suspended several times since 2000. Elections held in November 2003 to break the stalemate saw the extremist parties triumph at the expense of moderates.

THE DESIRE FOR PEACE

Despite the failure of the devolved institutions to work satisfactorily, there has been real progress in Northern Ireland. Many of the devolved ministers enjoyed great success, notably Martin McGuinness of Sinn Féin in education, and the different parties all contributed to policies designed to improve life in the province. Above all, the people of Northern Ireland have enjoyed the peace, the first since the Troubles began in 1969. Despite this, sectarian violence still flares up, usually around the contentious Orange Order marches that take place each summer to mark the anniversary of the Battle of the Boyne. Both the Real and Continuity IRAs still threaten renewed bombing campaigns. Neither the IRA nor the various loyalist paramilitary organisations have got rid of all their weapons. Paramilitary groups are still involved in criminal activities in order to keep funds rolling in, and still try to control their areas with intimidation.

But most people in the province want the peace settlement to work, and want the two communities to live together peacefully. The economic benefits of peace are enormous. The gradual relaxation of security measures, such as checkpoints and armed patrols, mean

THE COST OF THE TROUBLES

More than 3,600 people have died in the Troubles since they began in 1969. Of those, just over half have been killed by the IRA, with other republican groups killing 231. Among the IRA's victims are 465 British soldiers, 272 members of the Royal Ulster Constabulary and 133 targeted Protestant civilians. Loyalist paramilitaries have killed 990 people; 708 of them Catholic civilians. British government forces have killed 363; 145 were republican paramilitaries, 14 loyalist paramilitaries, and 192 civilians.

Over 1,500 of the victims came from Belfast and a further 500 from Co. Armagh, on the border. In total, 17,000 people have been charged with terrorist offences, and more than 40,000 injured, about three per cent of the total population of Northern Ireland. If such figures were applied to mainland Britain, 111,000 would have died and 1.4 million been injured, equivalent to just under half the British deaths during the whole of World War II. About one in seven of the entire Northern Irish population of 1.69 million has been the victim of a violent incident.

The Belfast waterfront today demonstrates the renewal that has taken place in recent years.

that Northern Ireland is coming to seem much more like the rest of Britain and Ireland, rather than the armed fortress it once resembled.

THE FUTURE

It is difficult to predict what the future holds for Northern Ireland. Although its population is still segregated - at least half of the people live in areas that are 90 per cent Catholic or Protestant - the advantage lies with Northern Ireland's Catholics.

The 2001 census showed that 53.1 per cent of the population are Protestant, and 43.8 per cent Catholic. But the Catholic population has a higher birthrate, and more Protestants than Catholics are emigrating to the rest of Britain and elsewhere. As a result, many republicans believe that time is on their side, and that eventually a majority will vote peacefully for a united Ireland.

THE ROCKY PATH TO PEACE

June 1998 First elections to devolved assembly

Aug 1998 Omagh bomb

Mar 1999 Power due to be devolved to executive, but deadline missed due to lack of IRA decommissioning

July 1999 Assembly meets, but Unionists fail to nominate ministers

Nov 1999 First executive under David Trimble takes power, but devolution suspended three months later

May 2000 IRA makes

significant move on decommissioning; devolution restored

June 2001 Sinn Féin outstrips SDLP for first time

Aug, Sept 2001 Two further suspensions caused by Unionist resignations to force IRA to disarm

Nov 2001 Devolution restored once more

Oct 2002 Fourth suspension of devolution

Nov 2003 Assembly elections see DUP and Sinn Féin emerge ahead of moderate UUP and SDLP

GLOSSARY

Boycott Refusal to deal with a person or institution, named after Captain Boycott, a 19th-century Irish land agent.

Budget Annual summary of income and expenditure of a country.

By-election Election held in a single parliamentary constituency or seat.

(British) Commonwealth International grouping of independent nations once colonies of Britain.

Catholic *see* Roman Catholic.

Constitution Written document setting out principles on which a country is founded and the rights its people enjoy. Constitutional action is political activity within the law.

Dáil (*doyle*) **Eireann** Irish parliament.

Democracy Government by the people or their elected representatives.

Devolution The handing down of power by the national government to a regional parliament or assembly.

Disestablishment Removal of official status from a national church.

Dissenters Protestants who dissent from the established church.

Dominion Self-governing independent state within British Empire recognising British monarch as head of state.

Emigration Movement of people from one country or region to another.

Empire Group of peoples or countries governed by one ruler.

General election Election in which every parliamentary constituency or seat in the country is fought at the same time.

Guerrilla Member of an unofficial, often politically motivated, armed force.

Home Rule Rule by the Irish parliament in Dublin, or the Northern Irish parliament in Belfast, under the British crown.

Internment Imprisonment of suspects without trial.

IRA Irish Republican Army.

Loyalist Person who is loyal to the crown of the United Kingdom; an extreme unionist.

Militia A body of citizens rather than professional soldiers, usually raised locally, used only in emergencies.

Minority Group of people who form a distinct but small group within a nation or organisation, who hold different views from the majority of the population.

Monarchy Country ruled by a hereditary king or queen.

Nationalist Person who is loyal or passionately devoted to his or her own country. In Irish politics, someone who believes in an independent, united Ireland, achieved by consent.

Paramilitary force Political army using terrorism to achieve its ends.

Parliamentary government
Government by elected representatives of the people.

Partition Division of a country into two or more parts.

Plantation In Ireland, the deliberate colonisation of Irish Catholic-held land with Protestant or Presbyterian settlers from England and Scotland.

Presbyterian Christian who is a member of an independent, self-governing Protestant church.

Proportional representation System of voting that represents political parties in parliament in proportion to the votes they receive in an election.

Protestant Christian whose church broke with the Roman Catholic church during the Reformation of the 16th century or was founded later.

Protestant Ascendancy Period of domination by Protestants over Irish affairs in the 18th and early 19th centuries.

Reformation Europe-wide revolt against the Roman Catholic church during the 16th century that gave rise to the Protestant churches.

Refugee Person who has fled from danger in one country to seek refuge in another, safer country.

Republic Country governed by an elected head of state called a president.

Republican Extreme Irish nationalist who favours an independent 32-county republic, achieved by violence if necessary.

Roman Catholic Christian who follows the authority of the pope in Rome.

Royalist Person who believes in government by monarchy, with a king or queen as head of state.

RUC Royal Ulster Constabulary, the Northern Irish police force. Its new name (since 1998) is the PSNI (Police Service of Northern Ireland).

Sectarian Narrow-minded or bigoted action by a member of a religious group.

Stormont Home of the Northern Irish parliament after 1932.

Stuart Dynasty of monarchs that ruled Scotland from 1406, and England, Wales and Ireland from 1603, to 1707.

Taoiseach (*tee-shock*) Irish prime minister.

Troubles, the Period of violence that began in Northern Ireland in 1969 and which continues to the present day.

Tudor Dynasty of monarchs that ruled England, Wales and Ireland, 1485-1603.

Unionist Someone who believes in the union of Ireland with Britain.

Veto Power to reject a proposal or stop something happening.

Westminster Home of the British parliament in London